# Loving Someone with Borderline Personality Disorder

*The Ultimate Guide to Caring and Loving Someone with BPD*

Tom Pete

# Table of Contents

# Chapter 1

# Understanding Borderline Personality Disorder

People with Borderline Personality Disorder (BPD) are described in this way by others, including mental health professionals. However, these labels are unfair considering the daily struggles that an individual with BPD faces.

BPD sufferers are similar to those who have 90% of their body burned in the third degree. They have no emotional skin, so even the smallest movement or touch causes them excruciation. BPD specialist Marsha Linehan explains this greatly misunderstood mental illness in these terms.

It is because of this severely damaged "emotional skin" that individuals with BPD are unable to control their feelings, actions, and thoughts. "Dysregulation Disorder" would actually be a more accurate and less derogatory term for this condition. BPD is a chronic pattern of behavior that starts in adolescence or early adulthood, just like other personality disorders. BPD differs from other personality disorders in that it is characterized by emotional, interpersonal, personal, behavioral, and cognitive dysregulation. What does this signify? To put it plainly, relationships have a significant impact on a person with BPD's behavior, sense of self, and capacity for functioning.  Self-harming actions and destructive behaviors can develop due to the fear of rejection or separation. Their negative self-image is caused by the absence of significant and encouraging relationships. They could have moments when they feel completely nonexistent.

A person with BPD might insist on spending a lot of time with their partner when they are first starting a new relationship. They immediately divulge the most personal information to one another in order to establish a deep connection. They will initially express their utmost love and respect for their partner. However, they will swiftly transition to feelings of rage and hatred if they believe their partner doesn't show them enough love, care, or appreciation in return. A person with BPD may exhibit excessive or inappropriate anger in this situation of devaluing their partner, which is often followed by strong emotions of shame and guilt. These emotions frequently feed into a belief that one is wicked or perverse.

Perhaps as a result, individuals with bipolar disorder, anorexia nervosa, depression, and borderline personality disorder are among the groups most at risk for suicide. Ten percent of BPD sufferers have committed suicide, and seventy-five percent have cut, burned, beaten, or self-harmed. These harmful actions that harm oneself are frequently a reaction to threats of rejection or separation, but they can also happen to validate one's emotional state.

## False Beliefs Regarding BPD

Misconceptions about borderline personality disorder (BPD) are common. It's critical to distinguish between fact and myth in order to lessen the stigma associated with this complicated illness.

**Myth**: It's just another term for bipolar disorder or schizophrenia.

- BPD is not the same as bipolar disorder, schizophrenia, PTSD, or any other condition. These conditions also cause some symptoms, like mood swings, but they are entirely different diagnoses.

- Owing to this overlap, BPD is frequently misdiagnosed; therefore, it's critical to receive an accurate diagnosis in order to determine the best course of action.

- Everybody has BPD symptoms. Anger is one of the symptoms, and we've all felt anger occasionally. That being said, the

frequency and severity of the symptoms are what characterize
the illness. For this reason, it's critical to get a formal diagnosis
and a thorough evaluation from a psychiatrist.

- Like most things, BPD can range in severity from mild to severe.

**Myth**: BPD is an adult-onset disorder.

- The DSM-5 indicates that it can be diagnosed in theory during
  adolescence, but a diagnosis shouldn't be made until the
  person's personality reaches the age of 18.

- Nonetheless, the disease can and does manifest in childhood.
  More than 60% of BPD patients in a study reported having
  symptoms prior to the age of 17.

- This is due to the fact that childhood trauma from events like
  bullying, domestic abuse, or disturbances is thought to be the
  primary factor in the development of the illness, along with
  genetics. While this isn't always the case, individuals with BPD
  exhibit elevated incidence of [having experienced] abuse. The
  likelihood of a person with BPD reporting having gone through
  trauma as a child is 13 times higher.

**Myth**: Life cannot be fully and completely lived by someone with BPD.

- This is completely untrue. The severity of BPD varies from
  person to person, as was previously mentioned, and the
  likelihood of improvement is greatly increased by seeking and
  adhering to appropriate therapy.

- Despite the fact that people often concentrate on the negative aspects, consider the positive traits that are also connected to it, such as creativity and passion.

**Myth**: Having BPD makes it impossible to have healthy relationships.

- Untrue. It is true that a person with BPD may have more unstable relationships if they are particularly sensitive to rejection or fear of abandonment.

- This does not, however, imply that they cannot have them or that their endeavors will fail. Thus, don't give up.

**Myth**: BPD is much more common in women.

- This one is not quite so cut-and-dry. Although it has long been believed that BPD primarily affects women, some research suggests that it affects men and women equally.

- Men and women typically exhibit different BPD symptoms: men are more likely to engage in self-destructive behavior and have angry outbursts, while women are more likely to experience high levels of anxiety and dramatic mood swings.

**Myth**: Individuals with BPD are merely attention-seekers

- This is a charge that is frequently thrown at individuals with BPD, particularly if they show signs of self-destruction or participate in harmful activities like substance abuse.

- Nonetheless, these behaviors are frequently a coping mechanism for uncomfortable emotions and ideas. Instead of "looking at me" to get attention, they can also be a cry for assistance.

**Myth**: There is no cure for BPD

- Fortunately, BPD is treatable and it's best to treat it as soon as possible. There isn't an instant fix, though. Treatments such as dialectical behavioral therapy (DBT), cognitive behavioral therapy (CBT), mentalization therapy (MBT), psychotherapies, and schema therapy are excellent. DBT is the preferred treatment approach for many mental health practitioners. Its effectiveness in dramatically lowering negative behaviors and hospital admission rates in individuals with BPD is supported by research.

- Medication is frequently advised to help manage mental illnesses, but since there is no approved medication for BPD, this is not the case.

- But occasionally, doctors will prescribe medicine to treat co-occurring disorders like anxiety and depression in order to help manage their symptoms. Effective therapy is ultimately the primary mode of treatment.

## Symptoms and Diagnosis

Typically, late adolescence or early adulthood is when borderline personality disorder signs and symptoms first manifest. A stressful situation or upsetting incident may cause symptoms to appear or worsen.

Symptoms typically get worse with time and sometimes go away entirely.

Any combination of the following variables may cause symptoms, which can vary in severity from tolerable to extremely severe.

**Fear of abandonment**: It's typical for individuals with BPD to experience anxiety when left alone. People with BPD often feel fearful or angry when they believe they are being ignored or abandoned. They might keep tabs on loved ones' locations or stop them from departing. To avoid being rejected, they might also push someone away before they get too close.

**Intense and unstable relationships**: Due to their propensity to abruptly and drastically change their opinions of others, people with BPD find it difficult to maintain healthy personal relationships. People have a fast transition from elevating others to an ideal and vice versa. Their friendships, family relationships, and marriages are usually turbulent and unstable.

**Unstable sense of self or self-image**: Individuals with BPD frequently experience feeling guilty, ashamed, or "bad" about themselves. Additionally, they might drastically and abruptly alter how they see themselves, perhaps by making sudden changes to their friends, careers, goals, or opinions. They frequently undermine their own advancement as well. For instance, they might purposefully fail an exam, sabotage relationships, or lose their job.

**Rapid mood swings**: Individuals with borderline personality disorder (BPD) may feel abrupt shifts in their feelings toward other people, themselves, and the outside world. Irrational feelings can shift quickly and frequently. Examples of these feelings include uncontrollable anger, fear, anxiety, hatred, sadness, and love. These alterations seldom persist longer than a few days and typically only last a few hours.

**Impulsive and risky behavior**: BPD sufferers frequently engage in episodes of reckless driving, fighting, substance abuse, binge eating, and/or risky sexual behavior.

**Destructive thoughts**: Individuals with borderline personality disorder may burn, cut, or otherwise injure themselves, or they may make threats to do so. They might also be contemplating suicide. They might also be contemplating suicide. A caregiver or lover's rejection, potential abandonment, or disappointment frequently sets off these self-destructive behaviors.

**Persistent feelings of emptiness**: Sadness, boredom, dissatisfaction, or a general sense of being "empty" are common in people with BPD. Self-loathing and feelings of worthlessness are also prevalent.

**Issues with anger management**: Individuals with borderline personality disorder (BPD) frequently experience extreme anger. They might use bitterness, sarcasm, or outbursts of rage to vent their rage. These episodes are usually followed by guilt and shame.

**Transient paranoid thoughts**: Severe stress, typically from a fear of being abandoned, can set off dissociative episodes, paranoid thoughts, and occasionally hallucinations. These are transient symptoms that are typically not severe enough to be classified as a distinct disorder.

Not every individual with borderline personality disorder exhibits every one of these signs. Every person has different symptoms in terms of intensity, frequency, and duration.

## Effect on Relationships

For someone suffering from borderline personality disorder (BPD), a mental illness that impairs emotion regulation, establishing and sustaining close relationships can be very challenging. Nevertheless, managing these relationships can be very challenging for partners, friends, family, and significant others.

On both sides of the equation, there is frequently a sense of helplessness and frustration. It is critical that we collaborate with all parties to improve their understanding of this illness and of one another.

**Those who suffer from BPD fear being rejected**
Almost everyone who has this illness finds it difficult to keep up with relationships. Even when rejection is inadvertent, they are acutely sensitive to it. BPD sufferers are afraid of being rejected or abandoned. For this reason, they might enter into relationships blindly or terminate them abruptly.

Many BPD sufferers find that these strong emotional shifts overwhelm them to the point where they act impulsively to feel better, like:

- *Overindulging in food*
- *Self-injury*
- *Abuse of substances*
- *Suicidal ideas or actions*

These fluctuations in mood could also happen often. A person with borderline personality disorder (BPD) may experience multiple mood swings in a single day, whereas most people experience one or two significant emotional swings per week.

People with BPD experience emotional ups and downs on a regular basis for years, whereas most people have periods in their lives when they are more emotionally vulnerable than others. Unstable interpersonal relationships with friends, family, and peers may arise from this.

**Causes of mood fluctuations**
By looking at the circumstances leading up to the mood swings, mood swings in BPD can also be identified from other kinds of mood disorders. In individuals with borderline personality disorder (BPD), mood swings typically follow an external trigger, which is frequently connected to being rejected or abandoned by another person.

*Additional outside variables could be*:

- *Actual or perceived rejection or abandonment*

- *Employment loss*
- *Breakdown in a relationship*
- *Severe incidents*
- *Trauma memories from the past*
- *Tension*
- *Insufficient sleep*

The fight-or-flight response of borderline personalities is easily triggered, shutting down the rational brain and triggering the survival instinct, despite the fact that researchers are still attempting to understand the brains of borderline personalities. As a result, they behave inappropriately or excessively for the circumstances.

Remember that your loved one's mood swings may only be one symptom of borderline personality disorder (BPD), even if they match the description above. Mood swings by themselves do not support a BPD diagnosis.

***Mood swings can also be brought on by the following circumstances or factors:***

- *Hyperactivity and attention deficit disorder (ADHD).*
- *Bipolar illness*
- *Alzheimer's*
- *Depression*
- *Changes in hormones*
- *Low amounts of blood sugar*
- *Side effects of medication*
- *The menopause*
- *PMS, or premenstrual syndrome*
- *Being pregnant*
- *Insufficient sleep*
- *Tension*
- *Abuse of substances*
- *Diseases of the thyroid*

# Chapter 2

# Causes of BPD

The main causes of BPD are genetics and adverse childhood environments; it is extremely unlikely that a person will acquire borderline personality disorder without the presence of one or both of these factors. Genetics and traumatic experiences in the past can combine to cause borderline personality disorder, a brain disease linked to a variety of neurological abnormalities.

Adult traumas can have an impact on individuals with BPD, exacerbating symptoms or making recovery more challenging. However, these traumatic experiences do not lead to the development of borderline personality disorder. Instead, a person's development of borderline personality disorder is the result of a confluence of hereditary variables and early life experiences.

## Genetics Factors

A person is five times more likely to receive a BPD diagnosis if they have a parent, sibling, or other family member with the disorder. Since borderline personality disorder is a brain disease, the presence of genetic factors linked to the disorder will undoubtedly alter brain development in a way that makes the individual more susceptible to BPD symptoms.

Childhood trauma, which happens when the brain is still developing and fragile, also plays a role in these harmful neural abnormalities. However, the effects of these environmental factors are amplified to varying degrees in individuals who have a genetic predisposition to borderline personality disorder.

2008 saw a thorough investigation of over 5,000 twin pairs by a group of European researchers working with the University of Missouri to ascertain whether environment or heredity played a greater role in the emergence of borderline personality disorder. Overall, they discovered that 42% of BPD symptoms experienced by research participants could be attributed to environmental factors and 58% to genetic factors.

A 2013 study that was published in the scholarly journal JAMA Psychiatry further supported the importance of genetic factors, which are far more likely to account for the consistency of symptoms experienced by BPD patients than any shared history of childhood trauma exposure. Self-image instability and relationship instability, two of the most prominent symptoms of borderline personality disorder, demonstrated a stronger correlation with these early environmental factors. Still, genetics plays a major role in its development, with heritable traits serving as the primary causative factor for the remaining core symptoms.

The onset of symptoms associated with borderline personality disorder is not caused by a single gene. Numerous genetic abnormalities are probably involved in the development of BPD, and these genetic influences may also make a person more susceptible to other mental illnesses like depression, ADHD, PTSD, bipolar disorder, and generalized anxiety disorder.

Those with BPD frequently have co-occurring mental illnesses, indicating the broad risk of mental illness linked to genetic factors and the alterations they induce in brain structure and function.

## Environmental Factors

Environmental factors also contribute to the development of borderline personality disorder; in this case, these factors include exposure to childhood trauma, loss, and neglect. Even in those without a history of abuse or neglect, only a small percentage of people will develop BPD, despite the possibility that genetic factors play a somewhat greater role.

Children are still going through a period of mental and physical transition, so anything bad can have a disastrous effect on their growth. Later on, a variety of mental health issues, including borderline personality disorder, might be diagnosed in them.

***The following is a list of childhood traumas that increase a person's risk of developing BPD as an adult:***

- *Abuse of emotions*
- *Maltreatment physically*
- *Abuse of a sexual nature*
- *Neglect by parents*
- *Parental divorce (abandonment or death)*
- *Observing abuse within the family*

Numerous investigations have examined the frequency of childhood maltreatment and neglect in adult individuals diagnosed with borderline personality disorder. The findings are startling: between 40 and 86 percent of those diagnosed with the disorder report experiencing sexual abuse, between 75 and 75 percent report experiencing emotional abuse, between 17 and 25 percent report experiencing severe emotional neglect, and between 75 and 75 percent report experiencing physical abuse.

When a child is not raised in a secure, caring, and supportive environment, as provided by their parents and other reliable caregivers, the long-term effects can be disastrous.

## Alterations In The Composition And Operation Of The Brain

Those with borderline personality disorder have brain abnormalities in both structure and function, according to extensive medical examinations. Because of these variations, individuals with BPD

- *Exhibit stronger emotional reactions*
- *Become emotionally unstable more frequently*
- *Difficulty controlling their rage*
- *Lack empathy and have a propensity to think negatively of others*
- *Respond to strange circumstances with dread and paranoia*
- *Go through periods of extreme stress*
- *Are prone to making rash and dangerous decisions.*

The combination of hereditary and environmental factors, life experiences that contribute to the development of borderline personality disorder is what causes the alterations in brain structure and function observed in individuals with BPD. Stated differently, the natural course of development of the brains of people with BPD has been disrupted by traumatic life experiences and genetic processes, resulting in altered brain structure and function.

From a neurological perspective, borderline personality disorder is largely determined by these alterations in the brain. People with BPD think, act, behave, and communicate in ways that are explained by differences in brain structure and function; if their brains had been constructed differently, they would not have received a BPD diagnosis. For this reason, BPD is no longer only regarded as a psychological disorder but also as a brain disease.

# Chapter 3

# Techniques for Communicating

Communication becomes even more challenging when one of the parties has Borderline Personality Disorder (BPD). Building a solid relationship can be facilitated by having a few communication techniques.

Has anything comparable ever occurred? Your spouse may be crying in the bathroom when you're cracking a lighthearted but playful joke about his or her cooking. Or perhaps you mentioned something in passing about a coworker's performance during a staff meeting, and a few minutes later, that person is threatening to quit.

Even though someone with Borderline Personality Disorder may have a great sense of humor, speaking ambiguously or with sarcasm can really confuse someone who has the disorder. Likewise, a person with BPD may have a tendency to see things through a magnifying glass if they exhibit even the tiniest hint of anger or displeasure.

Everybody can recognize and communicate the basic emotions of fear, pleasure, anger, and sadness. Someone who suffers from Borderline Personality Disorder could read something negatively if the meaning is unclear. Easily humiliated, insecure, and embarrassed, a person with BPD is prone to overreacting.

In order to prevent misunderstandings or confusion, make every effort to be as explicit as you can be with what you say and the message you wish to get across.

## Verbal Communication

*Try to stay away from the following forms of communication:*

- Launching an assault. When faced with a tight deadline, one may become irritated and bombard a colleague suffering from Borderline Personality Disorder with inquiries such as "Where are the reports I requested and the budget for next year? By now, they should be prepared." Make a thorough list and offer to go through it together, evaluating the status of each item, rather than approaching him or her in this hostile manner.

- "You" phrases. It's always simpler to place the blame elsewhere. On the other hand, criticizing someone who suffers from Borderline Personality Disorder might negatively impact their low self-esteem. So, try utilizing more individualized language rather than accusatory one. Rather than stating, "You forgot to pick up the kids again," for instance, you may state, "I guess you've had a busy day and forgot to pick up the kids." How about we arrange to meet at the end of the day from now on to determine who should take responsibility for that? In addition, is there anything you'd like to discuss about work?"

## Nonverbal Communication

There are situations when the impact of your words and delivery can be equaled by the way you carry yourself. To improve communication with someone who has borderline personality disorder, try utilizing these nonverbal strategies:

- *Maintain fist clenching and all limbs uncrossed*
- *Adopt a straight posture*
- *Push distractions aside, like a phone*
- *Wait to respond until you are certain the other person has completed speaking before exerting any effort or moving*

Managing someone who has borderline personality disorder can sometimes make effective communication seem impossible. If you are a manager, you may have considered terminating your staff member, and if you are a worker with a BPD supervisor, you may have considered quitting your position. The situation might get a little trickier if the person with BPD is a family member.

Regardless of whether your partner, coworker, or friend has a borderline personality disorder, trying these communication strategies could lead to a more fruitful conversation.

# Chapter 4

# Coping Techniques

As you move toward recovery, learning how to manage your loved one's borderline personality disorder can strengthen your bond. How you relate to your loved one can be greatly affected by learning about the illness, acknowledging your feelings, emphasizing accountability, streamlining your message, establishing boundaries, and taking threats of suicide or self-harm seriously. Love cannot "fix" borderline personality disorder (BPD); you must assist your loved one in getting treatment while also making time for yourself. Together, you can create a future free from your loved one's illness and pave the way for their recovery.

The illness known as borderline personality disorder (BPD) can be extremely overwhelming and appears to be entwined with feelings, actions, and interpersonal connections. BPD can appear to be an unbreakable barrier for family members of those who have the disorder to their loved ones. But, you can improve your relationship with your loved one and both of you get the help you need to heal if you learn coping mechanisms for dealing with the borderline personality.

**Acknowledge your emotions**
People without BPD are unable to relate to the reactions and intensity of emotions experienced by those with BPD. It may be tempting to dismiss their emotions as unreasonable or to try to talk them out of them. But for the individual suffering from the disorder, these emotions are very genuine. Thus, it is not only extremely painful but also ineffective to ignore their feelings.

You don't have to agree with them in order to validate them. Often, you can get great results by just repeating what they are saying. You could say, instead of "There is no reason for you to feel this way," "I can see you are in pain, it must be terrible to feel this way." Pay attention with respect, empathy, and kindness. For those with BPD, validation is so crucial that it now ranks among the most crucial aspects of therapy. Ensuring that your loved one feels acknowledged can significantly benefit both your relationship and your loved one.

**Make your message simpler**
People with a borderline personality disorder may misrepresent what you say to support their worst fears about you or about themselves, depending on how they are feeling at the time. Even if something you say is completely unintentional, it can still be construed as an attack. It could seem that the illness stands between you and your caregiver, obscuring your genuine intentions and preventing communication.

Keep in mind that when you converse with someone who has BPD, especially about delicate subjects, the emotion is probably so intense that neither of you is able to think clearly. Make sure each sentence is succinct, clear, and direct. Don't give room for misunderstandings.

Naturally, this cannot ensure that there won't be any misunderstandings, but it can help you communicate more effectively and steer clear of misunderstandings as much as possible.

**Promote responsibility**
It's common to find yourself taking on the role of caregiver when a loved one has BPD. It is, after all, only human to want to support someone you love and get things back to normal as quickly as possible. Nonetheless, instilling accountability can occasionally be the most compassionate action you can take. This isn't about abandoning him to cope with his illness on his own; rather, it's about fighting the impulse to shield him from the repercussions of his behavior.

Never try to fix something for him if he breaks it out of anger. Don't pay off his credit card debt if he accrues it. Allowing him to experience the consequences of nature may make him realize he needs assistance. By taking a step back and absolving yourself of guilt for things that aren't your fault, also enables you to cope with life more skillfully. Even though it may seem strange at first, you two can gain a great deal of empowerment from this.

**Establish boundaries**

Setting limits can initially seem wrong, just as encouraging accountability can feel wrong at first, as though you are betraying a loved one. Setting and upholding boundaries, however, can provide you both with the much-needed structure and drive. It can ultimately improve your relationship by making your loved one take responsibility for their actions and stopping them from putting up with inappropriate behavior.

When establishing limits, consider what will be practical and beneficial. Instead of making accusations and looking embarrassed, gently and lovingly present new ideas. If your loved one initially interprets you setting boundaries as a sign of rejection, don't be shocked if things get worse before they get better. Remain strong during these trying times; setting boundaries can be very advantageous for both of you.

**Never disregard threats of self-harm or suicide**

People with BPD frequently make threats of harming themselves or taking their own lives. Many people interpret these threats as manipulation and attention-seeking, particularly if their loved one has not yet shown up. Nonetheless, individuals with BPD frequently commit suicide and self-harm, so it is important to never discount the risks. Ten percent of individuals with BPD take their own lives, and despite common misconceptions, eighty percent of those who intend to attempt suicide inform others of their plans and even discuss them.

Don't call him or her attention-seekers or manipulators. Rather, accept that he is in great pain and stay composed as you express your concern for him. Stay with them until medical attention arrives whenever they threaten to hurt themselves. You should always take the necessary precautions to make sure your loved one is safe, even though it is never your fault if they attempt suicide or self-harm.

**Assist the person you love in getting treatment**

Individuals diagnosed with Borderline Personality Disorder (BPD) frequently exhibit reluctance to pursue treatment due to a multitude of factors, such as feeling that their emotions are legitimate or harboring bad memories of past interactions with mental health providers. Nonetheless, to bring emotional balance back and guarantee that your loved one has the assistance they require to make significant changes, professional mental health treatment is required. You might have to look for that treatment.

Residential mental health treatment programs provide the best environments for many individuals with BPD to start the healing process. These programs enable your loved one to receive intense therapy in an immersive setting, allowing for ongoing monitoring and quick progress toward wellness. With the help of a personalized program consisting of individual, group, and holistic therapies, the patient can start delving deeply into their illness and creating useful tools for changing their emotions and behavior. Making contact with a program that provides specialized trauma-focused therapies can be crucial to your loved one's healing process if they have experienced trauma.

**Seek out assistance for yourself**

For both you and your loved one, learning to manage borderline personality disorder is not simple. It's crucial to remember your own needs and feelings while trying to support a loved one with BPD, as many family members of those affected by the disorder struggle with extreme feelings of shame, fear, and isolation. Always remember to take care of your mind, body, and spirit by making time for yourself. You can obtain the support you need to manage by going to your own individual therapy sessions and/or making connections with support groups for relatives of individuals with BPD. Bridges to Recovery offers family programming that is specifically tailored for individuals just like you and is frequently an invaluable source of support.

# Chapter 5

# Assisting in Your Own Healing

Yes, you will probably be affected by your symptoms, and things may not always go well in your relationship. But it's crucial to remember that BPD is also a difficult mental illness to deal with. A person with BPD can benefit from having you in their life because you are a consistent and comforting presence. Here are some recommendations from people who live with BPD on how to effectively support others.

**Promote and comprehend treatment**

Although BPD is a difficult condition to treat, it is manageable. For this illness, there are specialized options like dialectical behavioral therapy (DBT). Assist the person you love to enter and/or remain in treatment. When receiving treatment, become fluent in the program's language and use it to provide assistance when needed. Learn the fundamentals of the four DBT skills—mindfulness, interpersonal effectiveness, distress tolerance, and emotional regulation, for instance—and how you can support a loved one in putting them into practice.

**Express your gratitude to the person you hold dear**

Because they want to be loved and validated in return, a person with BPD may go above and beyond to make you happy. When a person with BPD doesn't feel valued, relationships can become tumultuous: We begin to feel as though we hate [the people we love] because they haven't made us feel as though we've helped them or done what they wanted. By letting your loved one know how much you value the things they do to make you happy, you can help them fight this. If you experience love and genuine validation, be honest about it with people who have BPD.

### Expect conflicting messages

In a matter of hours, a person with BPD can go from idealizing you to being enraged and "hating" you (devaluing). They have a great fear that you will leave them, even though they "hate" you.

Be ready to provide consolation and meaningful reassurance when these fears surface by saying something like, "I understand that your feelings are overwhelming right now; I understand that you are afraid I will abandon you." However, I won't. I'll be there for you and we'll overcome this.

### Being in response

Being as responsive as possible is beneficial when someone with BPD reaches out to you. The person with BPD may feel rejected and internalize it as if there is something "wrong" with them if a friend or loved one does not reply. Everybody needs to love you and be there for you, as Katie puts it. If they don't, you begin to despise yourself in addition to blaming them. You begin to wonder, "What have I done wrong that they dislike me?"

Destructive behaviors and self-hatred may result from this. When faced with rejection or conflict, a person with BPD finds it extremely difficult to handle things because they punish and blame themselves. Because 75% of individuals with BPD cut, burn, bruise, bite, or injure themselves in some other way, this is one of the reasons self-injury is frequently linked to the disorder.

### Accept that it is not their fault

It is well known that BPD greatly strains relationships. A person may find it impossible or very challenging to control their symptoms in a way that doesn't negatively impact people who are close to them. Thus, keep in mind that you truly have no control over when symptoms appear. The hallmark of this illness is an inability to control or regulate one's emotions, thoughts, or behavior. Don't blame someone for having active symptoms of a mental illness any more than you would a loved one with cancer symptoms that interfere with day-to-day functioning.

# Chapter 6

# Treatment of Borderline Personality Disorder

Maintaining improved emotional balance during treatment requires upending maladaptive thought, emotion, and behavior patterns in the brain. Clinicians sometimes recommend a specific medication as part of a treatment plan. General psychiatric treatment (GPM), dialectical behavioral therapy (DBT), mentalization-based treatment (MBT), and transference-focused psychotherapy (TFP) are among the available treatment options.

## General Psychiatric Treatment

Providing most patients with "good enough" treatment is the aim of GPM or excellent mental management. In contrast to alternative medical services, this is not inadequate care. Studies have indicated that BPM can be just as successful in treating patients as DBT. In order to provide patient care even in the absence of more specialized or resource-intensive treatments, BPM integrates the essential components of other therapies.

## Cognitive-behavioral Therapy

There is a belief that DBT is the most effective treatment for BPD. Four skill sets—distress tolerance, emotion regulation, interpersonal effectiveness, and mindfulness—are given special attention. Users of DBT are able to lessen their negative habits and regulate their strong emotions. Patients can improve their self-awareness and interpersonal skills with DBT. Both adults and adolescents with depression and borderline personality disorder respond well to DBT treatment.

## Mentalize-Based Treatment

DBT seeks to help patients by lowering self-destructive behaviors and enhancing communication and interpersonal skills. You can better discern between your own thoughts and feelings and those of those around you by mentalizing your emotional state. Since people with BPD frequently struggle to recognize the consequences of their behavior, DBT places a strong emphasis on focusing on and reflecting on mental states in order to better understand how the mental state influences one's own behavior as well as the behavior of others.

### Transference-focused psychotherapy

TFP places a strong emphasis on the patient's sense of self and works to generate more accurate and cogent views of oneself and other people. If someone has BPD, their sense of self may be confused. TFP focuses on resolving issues related to identity, mood, social interactions, and self-esteem. TFP teaches patients to verbally express their feelings instead of acting on impulse, which improves interpersonal functioning and happiness.

Counseling, both individual and group, can also be beneficial. BPD is not always the main topic of discussion in group and individual therapy sessions because the subjects covered are so diverse. Group and individual therapy can address issues related to interpersonal connections, stress management, emotion regulation, mindfulness, and family relationships.

You may want to look into couple's therapy if your loved one refuses to admit that they have a BPD issue. In this instance, the relationship and encouraging improved communication are more important than your loved one's illness. It might be simpler for your spouse to agree to therapy, and they might even think about getting help for BPD in the future.

Encourage the person you care about to investigate healthy coping mechanisms for stress and emotions, such as mindfulness exercises and the use of deep breathing, yoga, or meditation. In the moment, sensory stimulation can also aid in stress relief. Once more, you can engage in any of these therapies alongside your loved one, strengthening your relationship and inspiring them to seek out additional treatment options.

Your loved one can learn to take a break when the impulse to act out or behave impulsively strikes by learning to tolerate discomfort.

It's critical to exercise patience and establish reasonable goals when aiding in your loved one's rehabilitation. Change is possible and does happen, but it takes time as with any pattern of behavior.

Rather than setting lofty, unachievable goals that will only lead to disappointment and discouragement for both you and your loved one, start small. You and your loved one will be more likely to succeed if you set modest goals that you can accomplish little by little.

Helping a loved one recover can be incredibly rewarding and demanding at the same time. You must look after yourself, but in the process, you can develop personally and improve your bond with one another.

# Chapter 7

# Seeking Your Own Support

One can easily become engrossed in heroic attempts to placate and please a family member or partner who suffers from borderline personality disorder. To the detriment of your own emotional needs, you might devote the majority of your energy to the person with BPD. However, this is a surefire way to lead to bitterness, melancholy, tiredness, and even physical sickness.

Helping others and having satisfying relationships are impossible when you're worn out and stressed out. The same rules apply as in a flight emergency: "Put on your own oxygen mask first."

**Avoid the temptation to isolate yourself:** Refrain from isolating yourself and give priority to spending time with loved ones and friends who bring you joy. People who will listen to you, show you that they care, and, when necessary, give you a reality check, are the people you need to support you.

**You are allowed to live:** It's okay for you to lead a separate life from the one you share with the person who has BPD. Taking time to unwind and have fun is not a sign of selfishness. In fact, you will both gain from the person with BPD's improved perspective when you get back into your relationship with them.

**Don't ignore your physical well-being:** Getting enough sleep, eating a balanced diet, and exercising can all be neglected when one becomes entangled in romantic drama. Make an effort to stay away from this trap. You can handle stress and maintain emotional and behavioral control when you're well and well-rested.

**Acquire stress management skills**: reacting to problematic behavior with anxiety or upset will only make your loved one more agitated or angry. You can learn to release tension as it arises and maintain composure under pressure by practicing with sensory stimuli.

**Remember the three C's rule**: Friends and family members of borderline individuals frequently experience self-blame and guilt for their destructive behavior. They might question what they did to provoke the person's anger, believe they are to blame for the abuse or hold themselves accountable for any setbacks in the course of treatment or relapses.

However, it's crucial to keep in mind that nobody is accountable for another person. It is the BPD person's responsibility to control their own actions and behavior.

*The three Cs consist of:*

- *I am unable to heal it.*
- *It wasn't my fault.*
- *It's beyond my control*

**Join a group for support**: Make contact with people who have gone through similar struggles and experiences.

The person who has been diagnosed with borderline personality disorder (BPD) is not the only one affected by the condition. Those who are closest to them are also greatly impacted, particularly family members. In response to these particular difficulties, support groups for families with BPD have become an important tool.

**Families are essential to the treatment of BPD**
Their patience, understanding, and support can make a big difference in how well a person is able to manage the disorder. But it's not a simple task. Family members frequently experience bewilderment, annoyance, and powerlessness when attempting to support their loved ones.

### The value of support groups for families

This is where BPD family support groups come into play. Family members can share stories, learn new things, and find solace in the knowledge that they are not traveling alone in these groups.

### A secure area to interact

The sense of community that a support group fosters is among its most advantageous features. Families can share their thoughts, frustrations, and experiences in these groups without worrying about being judged. Sharing like this can be incredibly relieving emotionally.

### Education resources

Support groups for education are frequently used as educational resources. Families can get additional information about BPD, its symptoms, and coping mechanisms through talks, presentations, and shared experiences. With this knowledge, they will be able to support themselves and their loved ones more effectively.

### Support on an Emotional Level

Taking care of someone you love who has BPD can be emotionally taxing. Support groups give people a safe place to vent, get therapy, and find solace from people who are aware of their particular struggles.

For families with BPD, there are both offline and online support groups available. Offline groups typically convene at health facilities or community centers. However, because of their accessibility and flexibility, online support groups are becoming more and more popular. Think about credible mental health forums and websites as well. To locate a support group, get in touch with local mental health providers and groups. They can frequently direct you to nearby resources.

Support groups provide a forum for information sharing, emotional support, and expression for relatives of individuals with borderline personality disorder. They offer a secure and encouraging setting where families can work together to navigate the challenges of BPD.

# Chapter 8

# Advantages of Having a BPD Companion

BPD is undoubtedly not a good thing. However, maybe there are benefits to dating someone with BPD. An intuitive, sympathetic, passionate, impulsive, resilient, creative, inquisitive, intense, intellectual, and brave person is among the many BPD sufferers. They are devoted to their partner and family and capable of profound love when not provoked.

They might overlook the vital, intensely personal, and happy parts of their relationship if they let the opinions of others and the Internet have too much influence over them. You will value your partner much more for who they are if you change your attention from the negative to the potential positive qualities your BPD partner may possess.

*The following are some positive effects that your partner's extreme sensitivity, empathy, and intuition can have on your relationship:*

**Elevated IQ**
Studies show that exceptional artistic talent and above-average intelligence (IQ > 130) are related to BPD. Your BPD partner processes information and solves problems faster than the typical person because he is incredibly intelligent. Because of his intelligence, he tends to be a loner and can get agitated easily if others do not grasp things quickly enough. They are also exceptional companions because of their rigorous analysis and insatiable curiosity. Talking with them broadens their perspective and engages them intellectually. A high IQ partner can also assist you in expanding your horizons and learning new things.

**They understand your pain**.
More than the average person, a person with BPD is familiar with pain, loneliness, and emotional suffering. Contrary to popular assumption, most

BPD sufferers are not empathetic people. Actually, quite the contrary is true—some of them exhibit "too much" empathy. They risk burnout if their empathic nature is not appropriately controlled and regulated, leaving them feeling overburdened all the time.

It's amazing how many people with BPD are able to feel emotions that they can't express. They may feel as though their partner can read their mind, even if they haven't expressed their feelings to them directly.

In one study, twenty-five participants without borderline personality disorder and thirty BPD participants looked at pictures of people's faces that only showed parts of their faces, namely their eyes. When it came to accurately identifying facial expressions, the BPD group outperformed the non-BPD group by a significant margin, indicating a higher level of sensitivity to the mental states of others. Your BPD partner will therefore be aware of your distress even if you make an effort to hide or deny it. Your BPD partner can form a close, personal bond with you because of their combination of acute intuition and profound empathy. This bond may even increase your emotional awareness.

**Address issues head-on**
People with BPD tend to be very driven to improve their relationships and solve any issues, which may be connected to their nervous attachment and intolerance of ambiguity. When conflicts emerge, they try to find the root of the issue rather than just brush them off. If you shy away from conflict, this might be stressful for you. The benefit is that you are compelled to address issues in your relationships head-on, communicate clearly, and resist the urge to become indifferent or avoid conflict.

**Creativity**
Many people have discovered a strong correlation between creativity and borderline personality disorder, even though empirical research has not been able to corroborate this association. They might be drawn to creative professions, have a strong interest in the arts, or have other creative traits. Several people with BPD may turn to creativity as a coping mechanism for

their emotional instability and distress. They can inspire you to express yourself and follow your artistic passions. It is ideal if your partner breaks up the monotony and infuses the relationship with the same intensity of creative energy.

**Parents who are kind and understanding**

While some individuals with borderline personality disorder (BPD) choose to pass on the trauma they experienced across generations, many are adamant about doing the exact opposite. After their partner has experienced a traumatic upbringing, they will find it difficult to keep their kids from following in their footsteps. You might be very good at using your grief as a parenting asset if you are prepared to put in the time and effort to better yourself via therapy and personal development. They will go above and beyond to meet their kids' needs and show them the love they were denied. Despite being less confident than other parents, they have the ability to be very receptive to their kids' needs. Furthermore, their spouse is probably going to respect their child's individuality, feelings, and goals without pressuring them to adhere too strictly to social norms. Your partner will probably support your child's ambition to pursue compatible career choices.

**Devoted and faithful**

Relationships involving people with BPD are often turbulent and intense because many of them struggle with emotion regulation. But in spite of their challenges, people with BPD frequently have a lot of love to give. Unfaithfulness is a possibility for some BPD partners, particularly if they behave impulsively when experiencing emotional dysregulation. But if they feel loved and safe in a committed relationship, most of the time, they will cherish the safe haven you have built and sought throughout your life. Your partner will be loyal to you and will make every effort to ensure the success of the marriage once they have committed to you.

**Reluctance**

Individuals diagnosed with borderline personality disorder are frequently perceived as psychologically fragile and incapable of handling challenges in life. Nonetheless, some people with borderline personality disorder have remarkably strong and resilient personalities (Paris et al., 2014). They have the ability to overcome hardships and difficult situations in life in a manner that most people do not. We will be astounded by their resilience when we consider the terrible traumas they experienced as children. Paradoxically, they can be remarkably calm when life-changing events occur, despite the fact that they frequently exhibit strong reactions to relatively insignificant everyday events. They might therefore be in the best position to assist their loved ones during a significant family crisis. People with BPD have shown that a person's life can be fully restored even after the most traumatic events. They can be an incredibly valuable source of support for others because they understand what it's like to be survivors.

**Fun**

Many people with BPD take pleasure in laughing with others and interacting with others. They are fun to be around because of their high level of energy and spontaneity. They have a tendency to act impulsively and take unnecessary risks. However, this can result in intriguing and memorable experiences if they are able to harness their daring nature in a healthy way and incorporate it into their relationship.

**Deep Passion**

Close relationships are very important to people with BPD. In addition to a love of people and a need for close relationships, this is partially caused by a fear of being abandoned. As a result, individuals with BPD frequently have incredibly passionate relationships. They will usually go to great lengths to strengthen their bonds and have a loving disposition. They might show you a lot of love, affection, and attention. This can be a welcome change if you've felt abandoned or alone in past relationships.

When in a relationship with someone who has BPD, people frequently notice that their emotional expressiveness gradually increases. You might also find it simpler to talk about challenging topics and express your feelings once your BPD partner demonstrates these abilities.

It takes courage not to be content in your relationships every single day. Overcoming adversity and surviving hard times are the ways that courage is developed.

# Conclusion

It's difficult to love someone who has borderline personality disorder. It can be painful to witness a loved one battle with intense inner turmoil, deal with a shaky sense of self, and experience such intense and unfiltered emotions. Even routine interactions can frequently carry a high risk of injury. The disease's intrinsic emotional instability can make you feel lost and uncertain about your situation and future course of events. You might experience a persistent sense of unease about when the other shoe will fall, even during times of calm. Will my voice tone be misinterpreted by you? Will you interpret it as a rejection? Is there going to be a conflict today?

It can be difficult to keep up a good relationship with someone who has borderline personality disorder, whether you are their partner, friend, or family member. In fact, there might be moments when you wonder if you really want to keep up the relationship. It's critical to understand how to love someone with borderline personality disorder in a way that both of you find stimulating if you want to forge a strong relationship.

Individuals suffering from borderline personality disorder (BPD) are not only challenging. They are not attempting to harm you maliciously. A lack of emotional resources to deal with intense emotions exacerbates psychological distress, which in turn leads to symptoms of borderline personality disorder. Occasionally, early traumatic experiences that interfere with the development of stable attachments and a coherent sense of self are the cause of this distress. But BPD is not always rooted in trauma; BPD can arise without an identifiable origin story. It is important to remember that, regardless of whether there is trauma or not, the feelings your loved one is experiencing are very real to him or her, even if they seem irrational.

Of course, having a relationship with someone who has feelings that have no basis in their own reality can be very difficult. You may feel like you're talking past the person you care about, or that your words and actions aren't registering the way you want them to. In fact, that's exactly what's happening. To have a healthy relationship, you have to learn to manage this disconnect between realities. The best way to do this is not to try to convince him that he's wrong; in fact, by doing so, he's likely to feel attacked and respond by pushing you away. Instead, learns to validate his feelings and acknowledge the reality of his experiences.

Validation, as discussed in a previous chapter, is an essential ingredient in loving someone with borderline personality disorder. Even if you disagree with or don't feel the same way as the other person, you must mirror their feelings in order to validate them. For example, if your loved one is upset because he or she thinks you're rejecting him or her, say, "I can see you're feeling hurt because you thought I was rejecting you; that must be a terrible feeling." This requires patience and self-control; it can be difficult not to rush in and try to convince him or her that you are not rejecting him or her. But it is essential to realize that the person has already felt the rejection, regardless of your intention. In a sense, he is suffering a loss that feels as real as if you had rejected him. If you allow her to feel her feelings and witness her pain without judgment, you will be showing her love and avoiding fruitless conflict.

However, don't dismiss your loved one's emotions entirely as the result of borderline personality disorder. Having BPD does not mean that someone cannot have legitimate complaints or that their feelings are always motivated by dysfunction. Acknowledge all of your loved one's humanity, reflect on what they are saying to you, and admit their mistakes if they make them.

Often, the person with borderline personality disorder can become the center of a relationship and there may not seem to be much room for you. Be sure to actively participate in the relationship. Express your own feelings, needs, and thoughts. Share your stories, your struggles, and your joys; after all, even if your loved one has BPD, he or she also loves you, values you, and wants to get to know you. An authentic relationship can only happen when both participants contribute to a meaningful social bond. Give yourself and your loved one the opportunity to do so.

At the same time, don't be afraid to set boundaries and communicate them calmly and clearly. At first, boundaries may be interpreted as a sign of rejection and trigger a fear of abandonment on the part of your loved one, but they are essential to ensure that your relationship remains healthy and guide you both on what is appropriate and what is not. Don't be surprised if your partner tests your boundaries to secure your affection; it's normal and motivated by deep-seated fears. Over time, however, your loved one is likely to realize that boundaries and love can coexist and that having boundaries does not mean he or she has abandoned you.

In the popular imagination, people with borderline personality disorder can sometimes be seen as fragile creatures incapable of taking care of themselves. The misconception is that borderline people are non-functioning people, but borderline people are often highly intelligent and intellectual people. In fact, most of the time they are very functional. Unfortunately, even intelligent people can fall into a save-save-self dynamic when borderline personality disorder enters the picture.

The emotional vulnerability of people with BPD can make it easy to believe that they need to be saved, especially in times of crisis. They may assume this role out of love, fear, or both. In turn, your loved one may come to see your rescue as proof of your love, temporarily calming their fear of abandonment as they become increasingly dependent on you. Meanwhile, you may begin to gain your sense of identity and worth from your role as a rescuer; it can feel good to be needed.

While this dynamic may initially seem consoling, it ultimately proves to be harmful to them both, in part because they have to constantly find something to be rescued from in order to receive their validation, worth, and demonstration of love. That something, in this instance, is borderline personality disorder. There is little incentive for healing when the symptoms of a disease become the site of communication and acceptance of love. In fact, healing itself may appear dangerous in this dysfunctional dynamic.

Fight the need to cut corners in order to avoid getting into toxic relationship patterns that impede healing, increase feelings of powerlessness, and incite animosity on both sides. Instead of taking on challenges on their behalf, acknowledge the skills and potential that your loved one possesses and assist them in realizing them. Tell him you think well of him and that you support him. Encourage him to become more independent rather than less.

Understanding that you cannot fix a person with borderline personality disorder is a crucial aspect of loving them. You are unable to heal their illness, but you can have a deep, meaningful relationship with them and provide them with priceless support. You can assist them in contacting top-notch treatment providers.

We now know that borderline personality disorder is treatable, despite the widespread belief that it is incurable. These days, skilled medical professionals employ a variety of therapeutic approaches, including trauma-focused therapies and DBT, to assist patients in regaining emotional and behavioral balance as well as long-lasting relief from BPD symptoms. For those with BPD, residential treatment programs are frequently the best choice because they enable participation in a variety of therapies catered to the individual's needs. Furthermore, the residential environment fosters the quick development of therapeutic alliances based on trust, which are crucial in the management of borderline personality disorder. Your loved one can learn useful coping mechanisms and put them into practice in a secure setting when surrounded by caring professionals and peers.

Naturally, developing more solid interpersonal relationships with loved ones is crucial to recovering from borderline personality disorder. Family and couples therapy are available in top-notch residential treatment programs to support you and your loved one during a joint healing process. You can discover unhealthy relationship dynamics, learn how to support your loved one, and lay a strong foundation for the future with the assistance of qualified clinicians. You two have the power to strengthen your bonds and build a happier, healthier partnership.